1896 · HENRY FORD'S FIRST CAR

ROBERT QUACKENBUSH

# ALONG CAME THE MODEL T!

## HOW HENRY FORD PUT THE WORLD ON WHEELS

PARENTS' MAGAZINE PRESS · NEW YORK

*For Piet*

*the boy who likes cars,*
*and with thanks to Tom Dana,*
*the man who knows them*

Copyright © 1978 by Robert Quackenbush
All rights reserved
Printed in the United States of America
10  9  8  7  6  5  4  3  2  1

Library of Congress Cataloging in Publication Data

Quackenbush, Robert M.
  Along came the Model T!
  SUMMARY: A biography of the developer of the
first lightweight, inexpensive automobile.
  1. Ford, Henry, 1863-1947—Juvenile literature.
2. Automobile industry and trade—United States—
Biography—Juvenile literature.  [1. Ford,
Henry, 1863-1947.  2. Automobile industry and
trade—Biography]  I. Title.
HD9710.U52F666   629.2'092'4   [B] [92] 77-10057
ISBN 0-8193-0952-4
ISBN 0-8193-0953-2 lib. bdg.

2

# ❧❦ PROLOGUE ❧❦

Sung to "Row, Row, Row Your Boat"

*On roads, lanes, highways, too,*
*Cars are on the go;*
*Merrily, merrily, merrily, merrily,*
*Ford helped make it so!*

1872 · HENRY FIXES WATCHES AT A WORKBENCH IN HIS ROOM

There was once a boy named Henry Ford, who was born and grew up on a farm in Dearborn, Michigan—near the city of Detroit. But Henry had no interest in being a farmer. What he really liked was doing anything mechanical. He liked to fix watches, repair tools, and take apart and rebuild toys to see what made them work.

Henry's father wanted his son to be a farmer. But Henry's mother was impressed by her son's natural bent toward mechanics. She asked her husband to build a workbench in Henry's room so that their oldest son could take things apart and put them back together after his daily farm chores were done.

HENRY MUST HAVE BEEN SMART TO FIX A WATCH.

ONE OF HIS FATHER'S FARMHANDS FROM GERMANY TAUGHT HIM ABOUT WATCHES.

1876 · HENRY SEES A STEAM ROAD-ENGINE FOR THE FIRST TIME

One day when Henry was twelve, his father took him on an errand to Detroit. Since there were no cars in those days, they went by horse and wagon. On the way, Henry saw a steam road-engine thundering toward them. He had never seen anything like it before. The machine moved by its own power—without a horse to pull it.

Henry ran to ask the driver all about the machine. The driver showed Henry how he shoveled coal to build up steam in the boiler. He explained that the force, or pressure, of the steam provided the power to turn the huge driving wheels. It worked like a train engine—except it didn't ride on tracks.

From that moment, Henry dreamed of building a smaller, lightweight horseless carriage that would not need so huge a boiler to make it run. He wanted to build a machine that could be driven by anyone, a machine that would move faster than any horse ever could. But first, Henry knew he would have to learn all about machinery.

1879 . HENRY GOES TO DETROIT AND WORKS AT TWO JOBS

As soon as Henry finished high school, he told his father he was leaving the farm to become a machinist. He went to Detroit where he found work as a machine apprentice.

The money Henry earned was not enough to pay for his room and board. He had to look for other work at night. Luckily, he found a job as a watch repairman in a jewelry store. He worked at the back of the store because the owner didn't want his customers to see that their watches were being expertly repaired by a sixteen-year-old boy!

In less than three years, Henry finished his machine apprenticeship and went back to the farm to help his father for a while. He also wanted time to work on some machine experiments of his own. He had not given up the dream of building an engine that could pull a carriage.

Henry learned that a neighbor had bought a steam engine, but the farmer couldn't find anyone to drive it. Henry volunteered for the job and was paid three dollars a day. Soon, word of Henry's skill in driving—and repairing—the machine reached the manufacturer. Henry was hired to sell and service steam road-engines all over southern Michigan. Also, Henry was often called to Detroit to repair machines of other manufacturers. One of these engines was an internal-combustion engine. It burned gasoline for fuel and was not as big as a steam engine. Henry quickly learned all about this machine, too. He wondered if a small internal-combustion engine would be right for his horseless carriage. He decided to build one himself and see.

1882 · HENRY IS HIRED TO DRIVE A STEAM ENGINE

Three more years passed. Henry married Clara Bryant, a girl he had met at a New Year's Eve party. Henry told Clara about his dream, and she encouraged him.

By now, Henry knew that others around the world were trying to make lightweight road carriers with gasoline engines. In the United States, Charles and James Duryea had already built a successful gasoline car in 1893. But only the rich could afford to buy these early cars, and many of them were badly built. The first cars were thought of as novelties, and few people took them seriously. But Henry Ford wanted to invent a sturdy, useful car that working people could afford to buy to provide faster and better transportation. So he and Clara moved to Detroit to be near the tools Henry would need to build his car.

In Detroit, their only child—a son Edsel—was born. A month after Edsel's birth, Henry burst into the kitchen where Clara was fixing a turkey. He was carrying a one-cylinder gasoline engine he had just built. He asked Clara to help him start it by feeding the gasoline. The engine worked! Henry was at last ready to begin building the car he had dreamed about!

WHAT'S A ONE-CYLINDER ENGINE?

A CYLINDER IS A PART OF AN ENGINE, SHAPED LIKE AN EMPTY JUICE CAN, WHERE THE GASOLINE EXPLOSION TAKES PLACE. THE LARGER THE CYLINDER—THE MORE POWERFUL THE ENGINE. THE MORE CYLINDERS—THE SMOOTHER RIDING THE ENGINE.

GAS

1893 · THE DURYEA BROTHERS INVENT A GASOLINE CAR — PROBABLY AMERICA'S FIRST

During the day, Henry had a job at Detroit's electric power plant. But in the evenings, he rushed home to work on his car. With the help of some fellow workers at the power plant, he made a car with a two-cylinder, chain-driven gasoline engine. It had a tiller—like a boat's—for steering, two forward speeds (but no reverse), and an electric doorbell for a horn. The car carried its three to four horsepower engine behind the seat. It had four heavy wire wheels that looked like bicycle wheels, so Henry named his first car the Quadricycle.

Late one rainy night, Clara heard a loud pounding behind the house. She ran outside and found Henry knocking down the walls of the shed where he was building his car. Had her husband gone mad? No, but he was caught in the classic inventor's nightmare: His car was ready to be tested, but it was too big to get through the door of the shed!

1896 · HENRY WIDENS THE DOOR OF A SHED TO TEST HIS FIRST CAR

When the shed door was wide enough, Henry ran inside and cranked up the engine by hand. Then he jumped up on the seat of his car and pulled back the lever to shift the engine into gear. With the engine sputtering, the carriage vibrating, and Henry bouncing up and down, the car moved out of the shed and down the road. Henry had done it! His car really ran.

Henry kept working at improvements for his car, such as a radiator to circulate water around the engine and keep it from overheating.

After three years, Henry was asked to design experimental cars for the new Detroit Automobile Company. Unfortunately, the company failed before Henry's designs were ready for production. He needed more time.

1897-98 · HENRY FORD'S QUADRICYCLE CREATES EXCITEMENT

1901 · HENRY FORD BUILDS A RACING CAR AND WINS A RACE

Henry was not discouraged. He decided to build a racing car, because auto races were becoming a popular sport and the best way to raise money to build cars. If Henry could win an important race, he would find people to lend him the money to make his dream car.

Henry's racing car had a twenty-six horsepower engine, including an improved carburetor and sparking system—called spark plugs. When the racer was finished, Henry entered it in a race at Grosse Pointe, near Detroit, before a crowd of eight thousand. Among the racing cars was a former prize-winner with a seventy-horsepower engine designed by Alexander Winston. Just before the race began, many racers dropped out. They didn't think they had a chance against Winston. But Henry stayed.

When the starting gun was fired, he and Winston were alone on the track. The two racers took off, with a mechanic hanging onto the side of each car to balance it. Winston roared far in the lead for several turns around the track. He seemed sure to win. Then suddenly, smoke rose from one of the cars. It was Winston's! Henry caught up and shot past Winston to the finish line. The crowd went wild! Now Henry knew he was on his way to having his own company.

After winning the race, Henry did find people to help him start an automobile company. But the new venture didn't do well either, because the investors really did not trust Henry's ideas about building a cheap car. So Henry withdrew from this company and formed another—the Ford Motor Company.

Within months, Ford's new company produced a low-priced car called the Model A. It had an eight-horsepower engine. Orders for the car came in faster than they could be filled. Now Henry knew he had been right. He designed other models, choosing a different letter of the alphabet for each, and orders poured in for them, too. Even so, the people who had invested money in his company did not believe a low-priced car would have lasting popularity. So Henry bought up all their shares of the company. And when he had gained full control, the first thing he did was to build a huge factory to make just one—and only one—car model: the fabulous Model T! And the world has never been the same since. The Model T, or Tin Lizzie as it was affectionately nicknamed, took the horse and buggy off the road!

1906 · YOUNG EDSEL FORD PULLS SLEDS WITH A MODEL N

Henry's Model T cost much less than a horse and wagon and was easier to keep up. Everyone wanted one—doctors, farmers, and traveling salesmen. It was a light, tough, low-priced car that was easy to repair, and anyone could drive it. Henry could produce them quickly because the main parts of every Model T were exactly the same. Even the color was the same—they were all painted black. In 1909, the Model T touring car cost only $825, and Henry wondered whether he could meet the sudden and overwhelming demand for his Tin Lizzie. By 1915, it cost only $440.

To speed up production, Henry installed conveyors to bring the Model T parts to the factory workers. "The work must go to the man, not the man to the work," Henry said. By doing this, his workers could produce the Model T faster, for the conveyor ended wasted motion. No longer did a worker have to lift, stoop, or walk to do his job. As the car moved along the conveyor, some men put on wheels, some put on doors, and others put on the engine. Each worker added his own piece to the car. In this way, the assembly line—modern industry's method of making many cars at one time—was born!

1913 · HENRY FORD DEVELOPS ASSEMBLY-LINE PRODUCTION FOR HIS MODEL T

1915·ONE MILLION FORD CARS HAVE BEEN MANUFACTURED

TIN LIZZIE REPLACES THE HORSE-AND-BUGGY

Millions of Henry's Model Ts were sold all over the world. Tin Lizzie became an important part of the American way of life. One Brooklyn minister even turned his Model T into a portable church. Roads were being improved and new highways were being built. Cities and towns were brought closer together. Henry Ford had started the automobile age!

As the cars poured out of the factory, Henry became aware that his workers were bored with assembly-line work. Many of his workers quit because of this boredom and new men had to be trained, causing production to slow down. So Henry made a bold move to keep his workers. He shortened the ten-hour workday in his factories to eight, and he more than doubled his workers' pay. Henry's efforts to keep his employees forced other factory owners to improve working conditions as well. Thus, Henry not only put the world on wheels, but he also helped to raise the standard of living for countless thousands of American workers.

1921 · THE STURDY MODEL T IS USED FOR JUST ABOUT ANYTHING

1927 · HENRY SADLY ENDS PRODUCTION OF HIS MODEL T AND MOVES ON TO NEW DESIGNS

Tin Lizzie lasted for many years. By 1927, when the 15 millionth Model T rolled off the assembly line, the touring car cost only $380. But the world had changed drastically since the first Model T. Other manufacturers, using Henry's methods of production, were making more modern cars inexpensively. Car buyers liked these newer models. The days of the Model T were coming to an end. When Henry finally accepted this, he agreed that the Ford Motor Company should unveil a new car. His Model A (named after one of his first cars) created a sensation. But never again would the Ford Motor Company be the leader of the automobile industry.

Today, manufacturers are still looking for ways to improve cars. The world energy shortage and the dangers of pollution have led to the production of smaller, fuel-saving cars. The cars of the future will have several strange-sounding new features: fuel injection, stratified charge, turbocharging. They will also be much lighter and more carefully designed to lessen air resistance. Many will be made of fiber glass.

Even so, Henry Ford will always be remembered as the pioneer of automobile manufacturers, the man whose mechanical genius changed the destiny of the world.

# HOW TO BUILD A MODEL "TIN LIZZIE"

- 2 styrofoam egg cartons
- pencil, paper, carbon paper
- sharp scissors
- tape
- white glue
- pointed toothpicks
- modeling clay
- black acrylic paint, brush or black spray paint

UNPAINTED MODEL

Trace or copy patterns. Put carbon paper under your drawing and re-trace it onto top of one carton. Cut out all pieces.

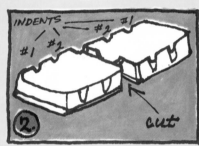

Cut the lid off second carton. Then cut lid in half directly at center. Notice indented sides for next steps.

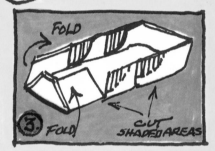

For car doors, cut out a quarter-circle at both indents on each side of half-lid. Also, cut straight down at first indent and fold in sides for hood.

Glue hood top in place and secure with tape. Then glue the dashboard behind hood and glue two seats in position as shown.

Make car roof out of other half-lid. Cut away sides, starting at back edge. Then cut across at second indent. Cut a small back window.

Put glue at one end of four tooth-picks and stick through roof side as shown. In proper position, tooth-picks spell NI. Repeat on second side.

DASHBOARD
(cut one)

FRONT AND BACK SEAT
(cut two)

PATTERNS FOR SEATS,
DASHBOARD AND HOOD TOP
(actual size)

HOOD TOP
(cut one)

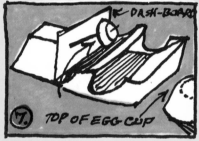

7. DASH-BOARD  TOP OF EGG CUP

8. GLUE AT BACK

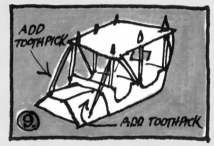

9. ADD TOOTHPICK  ADD TOOTHPICK

For steering wheel, angle a toothpick into dashboard. Cut top off one egg cup and stick on toothpick for wheel.

Attach roof to car body—one toothpick end stuck into each side of dashboard, two into each side of front seat, and one on each side just in front of back seat.

Cut off any toothpick ends protruding from roof. Then add two toothpicks, glued from front corners of roof to center of hood sides.

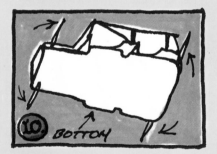

10. BOTTOM

11. CLAY FOR TIRES

12. CUT FOR HEADLIGHTS

For wheel axles, push a toothpick nearly half-way into each bottom corner of body.

Make wheels by cutting out four egg cups from carton. For spokes, stick three toothpicks crosswise through each cup. Roll a snake of clay around wheels for tires.

Push a wheel onto each axle. Dab glue on back where wheel touches body. Add accessories (i.e. headlights made from rubber pencilerasers). Paint your model.

Designed by Robert Quackenbush

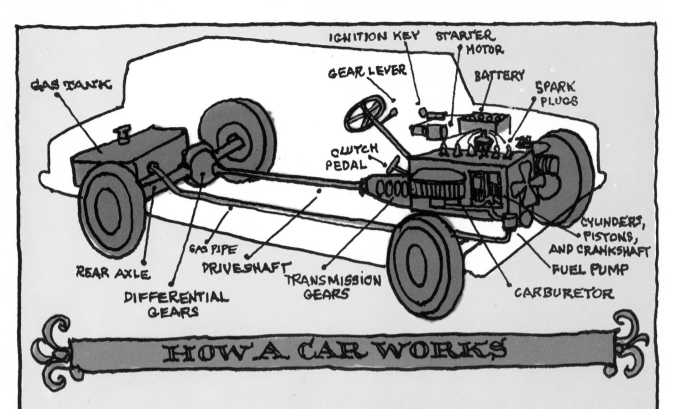

GAS TANK

IGNITION KEY  STARTER MOTOR

GEAR LEVER  BATTERY  SPARK PLUGS

CLUTCH PEDAL

CYLINDERS, PISTONS, AND CRANKSHAFT

FUEL PUMP

CARBURETOR

REAR AXLE

GAS PIPE

DIFFERENTIAL GEARS

DRIVESHAFT

TRANSMISSION GEARS

## HOW A CAR WORKS

On almost all cars, the front wheels are used only for steering. It is the rear wheels that are powered by the engine and make the car go. These eight steps show how the engine does this.

1. To start the car, the driver turns on the ignition key. This sends electricity from the battery to the starter motor, which is just powerful enough to get the engine going.

2. Gasoline is pumped from the gas tank to the carburetor by a fuel pump.

3. The carburetor mixes gasoline with air and turns it into a gas that gets to the engine's cylinders.

4. Spark plugs that are attached to the engine's cylinders set fire to the gas. The tiny explosion inside each cylinder forces down a tight-fitting piece of metal inside the cylinder called the piston.

5. The pistons have rods attached to them. When the pistons are forced down, they turn the crankshaft—in much the same way that your feet push on the pedals of your bicycle.

6. The crankshaft turns the transmission gears, and they turn the drive-shaft that extends to the rear wheels.

7. The driveshaft turns the differential gears that balance the rear wheels when the car is making turns.

8. Most important, the differential gears turn the rear axle, which turns the rear wheels so the car can go.

Whether a car goes forward or backward is controlled by the position of its transmission gears. The driver of the car determines this by putting the gears in the proper driving position: one of three forward speeds, or reverse. The crankshaft goes to work according to the position of the transmission gears. In cars with automatic transmission, the driver has only to push a lever or button; in cars with manual transmission, the driver must push a clutch pedal under the dashboard with his foot, and shift from one gear position to another by a hand lever.

There are other important parts to a car, such as the steering mechanism, a generator to store electricity, a distributor to pass electric power from the battery to the spark plugs, a radiator to cool the engine, brakes to stop the car, and windshield wipers to clean the windows when it rains. Ask your parents to show you these different parts on your family car.

CARS AND SLIPPERY HIWAYS TODAY